International Food Library

FOOD IN
JAPAN

International Food Library

FOOD IN
JAPAN

Jiro Takeshita

Rourke Publications, Inc.
Vero Beach, Florida 32964

Library of Congress Cataloging-in-Publication Data

Takeshita, Jiro, 1956-
   Food in Japan/by Jiro Takeshita.
     p. cm. - (International food library)
   Includes index.
   ISBN 0-86625-340-8
   1. Cookery, Japanese - Juvenile literature. 2. Japan - Social life and customs - 1945 - Juvenile literature. - I. Title. II. Series.
TX724.5.J3T297   1989
394. 1'0952-dc19   88-31465
                    CIP
                    AC

CONTENTS

AN INTRODUCTION TO JAPAN

Japan consists of a string of islands that range from north to south along the eastern coast of the Asian continent. Many small islands border the four main islands of Hokkaido, Honshu, Shikoku, and Kyushu, adding up to a total land area of nearly 143,000 square miles.

Japan is divided into forty-seven counties called prefectures, each of which elects its own governor. The governors represent their prefectures at the central government in Tokyo. Japan's head of state is the Emperor, who belongs to a dynastic line that can be traced back as far as 500 B.C.

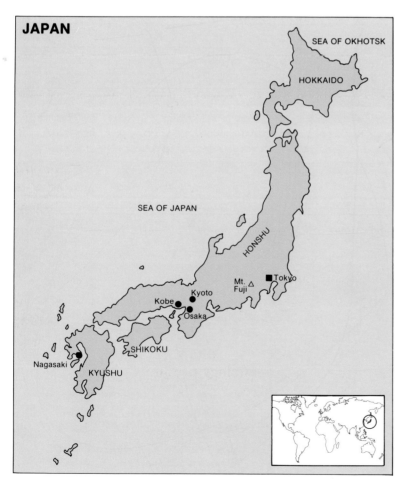

JAPAN

SEA OF OKHOTSK

HOKKAIDO

SEA OF JAPAN

HONSHU

Mt. Fuji △ ■Tokyo

Kyoto

Kobe● ●
Osaka

SHIKOKU

Nagasaki ●

KYUSHU

The snow-capped peak of Mount Fuji is reflected in a still lake on a beautiful winter morning in Japan.

The Japanese islands are very mountainous, with peaks rising to over 10,000 feet. Mount Fuji, over 12,000 feet high, is on Honshu, the largest island. Around four-fifths of Japan is covered by mountain ranges. Rather than live in the mountains, Japan's population of around 125 million is squeezed into the flat coastal areas. Most densely populated is the 5,000 square mile area along the Pacific coast of Honshu from Tokyo to Kobe. This area is home to half of Japan's people.

This part of Honshu is the economic and industrial center of Japan. One of the world's most highly developed nations, Japan is the third largest exporter in the world. Japan is the largest producer of motor vehicles in the world and ranks among the world leaders in shipbuilding, pharmaceuticals, electronics, and other high technology products.

At the heart of Japan's modern image, though, lies a wealth of tradition, rooted deep in the country's long history. Religion, philosophy, and art play an important part in all aspects of Japanese society.

AGRICULTURE IN JAPAN

Although only around fifteen percent of Japan is suitable for farming, the country is able to produce most of the food its population requires. Although Japan imports cereals, wheat, corn, and soybeans, the country is more or less self-sufficient in its production of rice, vegetables, fruit, meat, fish, and dairy produce.

Japan has few indigenous, or native crops. Most food crops have been introduced from Asia and Europe over the last 2,000 years. Rice, the first plant to be cultivated in Japan, has become a staple food crop. Other early crops included wheat, barley, millet, soybeans, and Japanese white radishes, or daikons. As European food has become more popular in Japan, the local production of onions, cabbages, tomatoes, cucumbers, and cauliflowers has increased.

Highly mechanized and efficient, Japanese farms are a model for developing countries.

Rice is often grown on hillsides in terraces like these in Tokushima.

Agriculture in Japan has changed greatly over the last forty years. After World War II new laws made it possible for people to buy the land they farmed. That meant farmers no longer had to pay overly high taxes to the landowners. In addition, crop prices came under government control, so the farmers knew they could always sell their produce at a reasonable price.

As farming became more profitable, people began to modernize their farms. They bought labor-saving machinery, used more fertilizers on the relatively poor, volcanic soil, and took an interest in new strains of crops. Although the farms have remained small, with only two or three acres of land under cultivation, they produce a high yield. Today, Japanese agriculture is highly mechanized and efficient, and has become a model for developing nations.

FOOD IN JAPAN

Traditionally the Japanese diet has consisted of rice, fresh fish, and vegetables. While these remain the staples, Japanese people today enjoy a great variety of locally produced and imported foodstuffs.

Fish is one of the nation's favorite foods, providing just under half the animal protein consumed by an average person. Only in the last hundred years have the Japanese begun to eat more meat and dairy produce. The Buddhist religion, introduced to Japan in 538 A.D., forbade the killing of animals, and the people ate no meat at all for over a thousand years. The Japanese still eat more than twice as much fish as meat.

A traditional Japanese diet is very healthy. It is high in vitamins and vegetable proteins, and low in fat. This balance has been changed by the recent introduction of more western-style foods, and the change has given some Japanese health problems. Even so, they eat only around a third as much sugar, fats, and dairy produce as people in the United States and the Japanese are among the longest-living people in the world.

In Japan's cities food-vending machines add to the fast pace of life.

Japanese people eat a lot of fish and seafood; here it is served in Japanese style.

A typical Japanese meal is made up of many small, artistically arranged dishes. Presentation is important. Japanese food must look as perfect as it tastes. Each dish is beautifully garnished and the table ware is carefully chosen to complement the food, which must be absolutely fresh and crisp. Often, each ingredient is cooked separately to preserve its natural flavor and texture.

Japanese people eat with wooden or lacquered chopsticks instead of with knives and forks. For an everyday meal in a Japanese home, all the dishes are served at the same time. They are placed in the center of the table and each person helps him or herself.

FISHING

With a coastline nearly 16,500 miles long and an ocean teeming with life, it is no wonder the Japanese looked to the seas for food. Fishing has a long history: archaeologists have discovered bone fish hooks dating back to the Jomon period (10,000 - 300 B.C.) No spot in Japan is more than 75 miles from the coast, and the plentiful supply of fish and seafood is always beautifully fresh.

Japan has one of the largest fishing fleets in the world.

Oyster farms are a common sight in the Japanese islands.

In the 1970s Japan was badly affected by new international laws governing fishing rights within 200 miles of some countries, where they had been allowed to fish freely before. Japan agreed to pay for fishing rights in many cases, and signed agreements with countries as far away as Portugal and South Africa as well as her closer neighbors, China, North and South Korea, and the U.S.S.R. With its fishing fleet scattered throughout the world's oceans, Japan is one of the world's leading fishing nations.

Many different kinds of fish are found in the oceans around Japan. The catches include herring, sardines, tuna, bream, prawns, eels, cuttlefish, and squid. Salmon, sea trout, and crabs are caught in the Sea of Okhotsk, to Japan's north. Modern fishing methods are used, and the boats are fitted with automatic controls and fish-finding equipment.

Although Japan does not have space available for freshwater fish farming on a large scale, certain freshwater species are produced in quantity. Saltwater fish and seafood culture has increased in recent years. Shrimp, lobsters, prawns, scallops, salmon, abalone, and octopus are now very successfully farmed, as are saltwater fish and oysters.

FRUIT GROWING

Japan first attempted to modernize its agriculture in the late nineteenth century. For the previous 250 years, the country had been closed to all foreign influences. When it at last opened its doors to the rest of the world, Japan began to look to the west for advice on farming methods, efficient production, and a supply of new crops.

The fruit trees imported from Europe and the United States at that time were disappointing. Japan's climate and soil were not always suitable, and many trees were attacked by pests that the farmers were unable to control. Most successful were the apple trees that were planted in northern and central Honshu. These flourished, and today apple production is second only to that of oranges.

Huge strawberries are one of a variety of soft fruits cultivated in hothouses.

Satsumas, a kind of orange, are the most important fruit crop in Japan.

Japan's most important fruits are oranges, said to have been introduced from China over three hundred years ago. These are a type of mandarin orange called *satsumas*, which are smaller and flatter than the large navel oranges. *Satsumas* are grown in the warm central and western parts of Japan. Many new orange trees have been planted since the end of World War II, increasing the area under cultivation to over 340,000 acres. Production stands at around 3 million tons each year, of which 25 to 30 percent is canned or blended with other oranges to make juice.

In addition to apples and oranges, Japan produces a variety of fruits including persimmons, Japanese pears, and chestnuts that are native to the islands. Cherries, strawberries, pineapples, grapes, peaches and plums are also widely cultivated.

REGIONAL COOKING

Japanese cooking does not show as much regional variation as some other countries, although many places have their specialties. The city of Kyoto in south Honshu is one of Japan's great cultural centers. It is famous for its vegetarian dishes, in which bean curd is prepared in many different ways.

The accessible port of Nagasaki on the west coast of the southern island of Kyushu was once Japan's main sea trading center. Here the Chinese, Korean, and Portuguese ships used to dock, bringing their wares and a little of their way of life. Chinese culinary influences are still evident in the area, and a cake introduced by the Portuguese is a local specialty.

Tokyo and Osaka, meanwhile, specialize in seafood and various kinds of seaweed that the Japanese cultivate in quantity. In these cities one can also experience top quality Japanese formal dining, called *kaiseki ryori*.

Sushi, a selection of raw fish, is a popular dish in Japan.

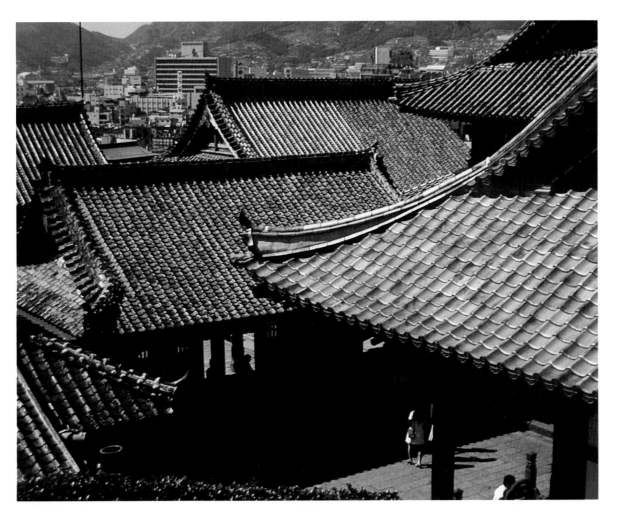

The old city of Kyoto, a great cultural center, is famous for its vegetarian cooking.

Guests must first remove their shoes and put on a pair of light slippers before entering the dining room. To our western eyes the room appears bare of furnishings, with a floor made of straw matting called tatami. After removing their slippers, the diners take their places, either kneeling or cross-legged, on thick cushions around a low table. The seven to twelve dishes are served in an order dictated by hundreds of years of tradition, and with garnishes reflecting the season of the year. This kind of dining is very expensive, and is much less common in Japan today than it used to be.

Wherever one travels in Japan, though, green tea is the most common and popular drink. Its delicate flavor is a perfect accompaniment to the light, fresh Japanese cuisine.

17

JAPANESE FESTIVALS

Japan is a land of many festivals, most of which are held only in one town to commemorate a great event or revered person connected with the area. Some days, like the spring and fall equinoxes in March and September, are national holidays and are celebrated everywhere in Japan. In one week at the end of April and beginning of May, the Japanese celebrate three festivals: The Emperor's Birthday, Constitution Day, and Children's Day. This week has been called Golden Week, and many people take vacations at that time. The most important national holiday in Japan is New Year. Families spend as much time together as they can, observing all the traditions relating to feasting, visiting, and playing games. The festivities usually last for several days.

The Gion Festival, Kyoto, Japan.

The Imperial Palace in Tokyo is the home of Japan's Emperor.

All four seasons are welcomed with celebrations as thoughtful as they are colorful. At the time of the spring and fall equinoxes, which coincide with the Buddhist festival of Higan, Japanese people visit and decorate their family graves with flowers in honor of their ancestors.

One of Japan's best known local festivals takes place in the city of Kyoto during the month of July. Called the Gion Festival, it commemorates the lifting of a terrible plague that killed many of Kyoto's inhabitants in the ninth century. The highlight of the festival takes place on July 17 each year. A procession of huge floats showing scenes from classical Japanese literature, legend, and history, as well as Chinese philosophy and Buddhism, winds through the streets of Kyoto. Vivid costumes, ancient music played on flutes and drums, and beautifully styled fans, all attest to the brilliance of Japan's traditional heritage.

A FESTIVE MENU FOR A FAMILY OCCASION

Prawn And Watercress Soup
Boiled Rice
Chicken Teriyaki
Eggplant With Sesame Seeds
Tuna Fish And Cucumber Salad
Grilled Mushrooms
Fresh Fruit

Family dinner parties are much less formal than the *kaiseki ryori* style of dining described in Chapter 7. Arrange individual bowls of boiled rice to the left of each place setting. Serve the soup, eggplant, tuna fish, and mushroom dishes individually in bowls or on small plates. The chicken teriyaki main dish should be presented in a large serving dish, garnished with scallions, so that each person can help him or herself. This meal is designed to serve six people.

Prawn And Watercress Soup

  6 *cups dashi stock*
  1 *tablespoon shoyu*
12 *cooked prawns*
  1 *bunch watercress, coarsely chopped*
  4 *tablespoons cornstarch*
    pinch salt

1. Pour the dashi stock, shoyu, and salt into a pan and bring to a boil.
2. Divide the prawns and watercress among the six soup bowls. Pour on the boiling stock, and serve hot.

Chicken Teriyaki

6 *pieces of boned chicken breast*
¾ *cup shoyu*
1 *tablespoon fresh ginger root, minced*
1 *teaspoon garlic, minced*
4 *tablespoons oil*
1 *teaspoon sugar*

1. Slice the chicken breasts and place in a dish.
2. Mix the shoyu, garlic, sugar, and ginger and pour over the chicken. Let marinate for 30 minutes, and then remove the chicken. Save the liquid.
3. Heat the oil in a large pan and gently fry the chicken slices for 5 to 10 minutes, until cooked.
4. Drain off any excess oil and pour the marinade over the chicken in the pan. Simmer for 5 minutes and serve hot.

Smaller grilled mushrooms can be attractively presented as shown in this photograph.

Eggplant With Sesame Seeds

   2 large eggplants
   2 teaspoons roasted sesame seeds
   ¼ cup shoyu

1. Wash and dry the eggplants, then place them on a in the center of an oven preheated to 475 degrees. Cook for 30 minutes, turning every few minutes.
2. Pour the shoyu into 6 small bowls, one per person.
3. Remove the eggplants from the oven, cool and peel away the skin. Cut into ¼-inch thick slices and divide among the six serving plates. Sprinkle with sesame seeds, and serve with the shoyu.

Tuna Fish Salad

   1 head of lettuce
   6 radishes, thinly sliced
   ½ cup shredded cucumber
   6 tablespoons vinegar
   1 tablespoon shoyu
   1 small can tuna fish

1. Arrange the lettuce, radishes, and cucumber in a serving bowl. Place the tuna fish on top of the salad vegetables.
2. Mix together the vinegar and shoyu. Pour over the salad and tuna fish and serve.

Grilled Mushrooms

   6 large fresh mushrooms
   4 tablespoons shoyu

1. Wash mushrooms and trim off the end of the stems.
2. Pour the shoyu over the mushrooms. Let marinate for one hour, and then drain.
3. Place the mushrooms in an ovenproof pan and broil for 2 minutes on each side, brushing with a little of the marinade. Serve on individual plates.

Tuna Fish Salad.

A VEGETARIAN MEAL

Vegetable Tempura With Tentsuyu Sauce
Boiled Rice

Many Japanese people are vegetarians, and Japanese cooking uses many different kinds of vegetables. Place a bowl of boiled rice to the left of each place setting before serving the tempura and tentsuyu sauce. Each person mixes some daikon and ginger with the sauce, and dips the vegetable pieces into the sauce mixture.

Vegetable Tempura

  4 *medium mushrooms, whole*
  4 *strips green pepper, 1 inch × 2 inches*
  4 *round slices eggplant, ¼ inch thick*
  4 *round slices peeled potato, ¼ inch thick*
  4 *small pieces bamboo shoot*
  3 *cups vegetable oil*

For batter:
  1 *egg*
  ¾ *cup flour*
  ¼ *cup cornstarch*
  ½ *cup water*

For garnish:
  2 *inch piece daikon, grated*
  1 *inch piece root ginger, grated*
  1 *lime, cut into 8 wedges*

1. Make the batter by beating the egg and adding the water. Mix the flour and cornstarch together and slowly add to the egg. Don't worry if the mixture is a little lumpy.
2. Pour the vegetable oil into a deep pan and heat for a few minutes.
3. Dip one of the vegetable pieces into the batter mixture and place in a ladle or large spoon. Dip the ladle containing the batter-covered vegetable into the hot oil for about 2 minutes, or until crisp and light brown. Remove the vegetable to a warm plate covered with absorbent paper towels.

A tray of tempura, including shrimp and a variety of vegetables.

4. Repeat step 3 for each piece of vegetable. Serve immediately on a large plate, garnished with lime, grated root ginger and daikon, and tentsuyu sauce.

Tentsuyu Sauce

   1 cup instant dashi stock
   ¼ cup shoyu

1. Mix the ingredients together and bring to a boil in a pan.
2. Pour into individual dishes and serve with the tempura.

25

A NON-VEGETARIAN MEAL

Broiled Fish With Shoyu
Boiled Rice
Pickled Cabbage Salad

Japanese people are very fond of fish, which are plentiful in the ocean surrounding their islands. This fish meal is designed for four people. Serve the fish and rice first, followed by the salad.

Broiled Fish With Shoyu

1 large (2-3 lbs.) snapper, sole, or bass
½ cup shoyu
1 tablespoon vegetable oil

1. Using a sharp knife, cut diagonally into each side of the fish to make a crisscross pattern.
2. Pour the oil and shoyu over the fish and marinate for 30 minutes.
3. Place under a preheated broiler and cook for 7 minutes each side, or until the flesh is firm. Serve hot.

Pickled Cabbage Salad

1 Chinese cabbage
4 tablespoons sesame seeds
½ cup vinegar
4 tablespoons sugar
1 teaspoon salt

1. Mix together the vinegar, sugar, and salt in a pan and bring the mixture to a boil. Remove from heat and let cool.
2. Meanwhile, cut the cabbage into thin strips and place in a bowl.
3. When the vinegar mixture has cooled, pour it over the cabbage. Place a plate inside the bowl to cover the cabbage and press down firmly. Put a heavy object on top of the plate and let stand at least one hour.
4. Sprinkle with the sesame seeds before serving.

Broiled Fish With Shoyu.

AN EVERYDAY MEAL

In Japan rice is served with every meal. The Japanese always use short or medium-grain rice in their cuisine. In the following recipe leftover cooked chicken breast is mixed with rice to make a quick and tasty lunch for four.

Japanese Chicken Rice

- ½ *lb. cooked chicken breast, boned*
- 6 *tablespoons shoyu*
- 5 *cups chicken stock*
- 2½ *cups medium-grain rice*
- 1 *cup cooked peas*
- 1 *cup button mushrooms,*
  cut into quarters
- 2 *large tomatoes, chopped*

1. Slice the cooked chicken breast and place in a bowl.
2. Pour the shoyu over the chicken. Let marinate for 20 minutes.
3. When the chicken is ready, remove it from the marinade into a large pan and add the chicken stock. Bring the mixture to a boil and add the rice. Cover and cook gently for 20 minutes.
4. Stir in the peas, mushrooms, and tomatoes.
5. When the rice has absorbed all the liquid, remove it from the pan and divide it into four bowls. Place the marinated chicken on top.

GLOSSARY OF COOKING TERMS

For those readers who are less experienced in the kitchen, the following list explains the cooking terms used in this book.

Boned	Having had the bones removed
Chopped	Cut into small pieces measuring about ½ inch
Garnish	Decorate
Grated	Rubbed against a grater to produce very small pieces
Marinated	Covered with a mixture of juices, called a marinade, and left to soak
Minced	Chopped into tiny pieces or put through a mincer
Seeded	Having had the seeds removed
Preheated	Already heated to the required temperature
Simmer	The lowest setting on a stove, usually marked
Sliced	Cut into pieces that show part of the original shape of the vegetable
Thinly sliced	As above, but thinner
Spoon measurements	Tablespoons and teaspoons should be filled only to the level of the spoon's edge, not heaped.

JAPANESE COOKING

To make the recipes in this book, you will need the following special ingredients:

Bamboo shoots This vegetable can be bought canned at any large supermarket.

Chicken stock This can be bought in cans in the soup section of all supermarkets. You may substitute an instant broth or homemade stock, if it is on hand in your kitchen.

Daikon These radishes, pronounced DYE kon, are one of the most commonly used vegetables in Japan. They are now carried in the produce section of many supermarkets.

Dashi stock Dashi stock is made from dried bonito, a variety of tuna. You may find packets of dashi stock or dashi-no-moto at stores that specialize in oriental foods. Otherwise, substitute a fish-flavored bouillon cube.

Garnishes It is important that Japanese food is artistically presented. Use any kinds of vegetables to make attractive garnishes for your dishes.

Ginger root Fresh ginger can be bought at most large supermarkets.

Oil Use only light vegetable oils, such as sunflower oil.

Rice Use only short or medium-grain rice.

Sesame seeds These seeds can be bought at a supermarket in the spice section.

Shoyu This Japanese light soy sauce is carried by many large supermarkets. Do not use dark soy sauce, which ruins the delicate flavor of the food.

Japanese oyster boat work.

31

INDEX

We would like to thank and acknowledge the following people for the use of their photographs and transparencies:

Bruce Coleman Ltd (Orion Press): 7; Japan National Tourist Organization: Cover, T/Page, 8/9, 10/11, 16/24, 25, 18, 19; Japan Information Center: 15, 29, 30; Octopus Publishing Group — Peter Myers: 27, 28 — James Murphy: 21, 23.